KT-116-346

# KEY TO MAPS

| | |
|---|---|
| **PERU** | Country name |
| ~~~~~~ | Country border |
| ■ | More than 1 million people* |
| ● | More than 500,000 people |
| • | Less than 500,000 people |
| □ | Country capital |
| ANDES MTS | Mountain range |
| ▲ Aconcagua 6960m | Mountain with its height |

| | |
|---|---|
| Paraná | River |
| | Canal |
| | Lake |
| | Dam |
| | Island |

| | |
|---|---|
| | Forest |
| | Crops |
| | Dry grassland |
| | Desert |
| | Tundra |
| | Polar |

*Population figures in all cases are estimates, based on the most recent censuses where available or a variety of other sources.*

## CONTINENT CLOSE-UPS

### SOUTH AMERICA

**People and Beliefs** Map of population densities; chart of percentage of population per country and country areas; panel on people and religion; map of main languages and endangered peoples.

**Climate and Vegetation** Map of vegetation; chart of land use; maps of temperature and rainfall.

**Ecology and Environment** Map and panel on environmental damage to land and sea; map, panel and diagram on volcanoes and other natural hazards; panel on endangered species.

**Economy** Map of products; chart and panel on gross and per capita domestic products; map of energy sources.

**Politics and History** Panel and timeline of great events; map of colonies and dates of independence; map of important historical events.

### ANTARCTICA

**Antarctica and Islands** Map centred on South Pole showing location of continent and islands; panels, globes and illustrations.

**Antarctica and its Exploration** Map showing routes of explorers; panel of important dates; map of research stations.

**Antarctica Today** Map showing areas claimed by various nations; maps of winter and summer temperatures and pack-ice limits; map of mineral resources; map of the ozone hole; panel on conservation as a World Park.

---

**Index** All the names on the maps and in the picture captions can be found in the index at the end of the book.

# CONTENTS

Giant anteater, see page 21

# SOUTH AMERICA

South America, the fourth largest continent, covers about 12 per cent of the world's land area. It contains the world's longest mountain range and the world's largest rainforest. The countries of South America contain rich farmland and many other resources, but they are far less developed than Canada and the United States in North America.

Argentina, Brazil, Chile and Venezuela are the most prosperous countries. Seven independent countries are classed as lower middle-income countries and Guyana is the poorest country. South America's population includes Native Americans (Amerindians) and people of European and black African origin. Many people are of mixed descent.

*PACIFIC OCEAN*

**Simón Bolívar** (1783-1830) was a South American general. His victories won independence for Bolivia, Colombia, Ecuador, Peru and Venezuela. Spain and Portugal ruled much of South America between the early 16th and early 19th centuries.

**Andean condors** are large vultures found in the Andes Mountains. The Andes stretch from Colombia and Venezuela to Cape Horn at the southern tip of South America. They form the world's longest mountain range above sea level.

VENEZUELA

Angel Falls

GUY

*Guiana Highla*

COLOMBIA

ECUADOR

*Amazon Bas*

*ANDES*

PERU

*Atacama Desert*

BOLIVIA

*MOUNTAINS*

PARAGU

CHILE

▲ *Aconcagua 6960m*

ARGENTINA

Falkland Islands (U

*Cape Horn*

CONTINENTS IN CLOSE-UP

# SOUTH AMERICA AND ANTARCTICA

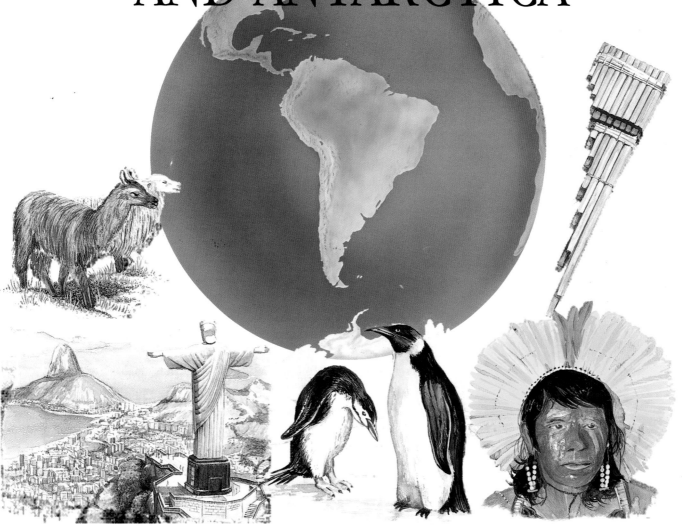

## MALCOLM PORTER and KEITH LYE

CHERRYTREE BOOKS

Designed and produced by
AS Publishing
Text by Keith Lye
Illustrated by Malcolm Porter and Raymond Turvey

New edition published 2008 by
Cherrytree Books, part of the
Evans Publishing Group
2a Portman Mansions
Chiltern Street
London W1U 6NR

Copyright © Malcolm Porter and AS Publishing

British Library Cataloguing in Publication data

Porter, Malcolm
    South America. - (Continents in close-up)
    1.Children's atlases
    2.South America - Maps for children
    I.Title II.Lye, Keith
    912.8

ISBN 978 1842344590

Printed in Spain by Grafo SA

# CONTINENTS IN CLOSE-UP
# SOUTH AMERICA
## AND ANTARCTICA

This illustrated atlas combines maps, pictures, flags, globes, information panels, diagrams and charts to give overviews of the continents of South America and Antarctica and a closer look at the countries of South America.

## COUNTRY CLOSE-UPS

Each double-page spread has these features:

**Introduction** The author introduces the most important facts about the country or region.

**Globes** A globe on which you can see the country's position in the continent and the world.

**Flags** Every country's flag is shown.

**Information panels** Every country has an information panel which gives its area, population and capital, and where possible its other main towns, languages, religions, government and currency.

**Pictures** Important features of each country are illustrated and captioned to give a flavour of the country. You can find out about physical features, famous people, ordinary people, animals, plants, places, products and much more.

**Maps** Every country is shown on a clear, accurate map. To get the most from the maps it helps to know the symbols which are shown in the key on the opposite page.

**Land** You can see by the colouring on the map where the land is forested, frozen or desert.

**Height** Relief hill shading shows where the mountain ranges are. Individual mountains are marked by a triangle.

**Direction** All of the maps are drawn with north at the top of the page.

**Scale** All of the maps are drawn to scale so that you can find the distance betweeen places in miles or kilometres.

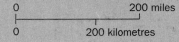

**SOUTH AMERICA**
**Area**: 17,832,000sq km (6,885,000sq miles)
**Population**: 375,566,000
**Number of independent countries**: 12

**SURINAM**
**FRENCH GUIANA**

*ATLANTIC OCEAN*

**Angel Falls**, in eastern Venezuela, is the world's highest waterfall. It has a total height of 979m (3,212ft) and a longest single drop of 807m (2,648ft). The highlands of eastern Venezuela form part of the Guiana Highlands.

**B R A Z I L**

*Brazilian Highlands*

miles
0 — 500
0 — 500
kilometres

**Rainforests** cover a huge area of northern South America. Much of the forest lies in the Amazon basin, a vast area drained by the River Amazon and its many tributaries. Large areas of forest are being cut down.

**RUGUAY**

**Llamas** are domesticated members of the camel family. The people of the Andes use them to carry goods and make their wool into warm clothing. Llamas do not drink much. They get moisture from the grasses and low shrubs that grow in mountain areas.

**Brasília** is the capital of Brazil. Building began in a former wilderness area in the 1950s. The city became the official capital in 1960 and is famous for its modern buildings. Its population is small compared with those of Rio de Janeiro and São Paulo. Brazil is South America's largest country.

# VENEZUELA

Venezuela faces the Caribbean Sea, which is part of the Atlantic Ocean. The explorer Christopher Columbus, on his third voyage sailing for Spain, landed on the coast in 1498. Venezuela declared itself independent of Spain in 1811.

The country is one of the world's top ten producers of oil and this has helped it to develop its economy. Venezuela is one of the more prosperous countries in South America. But, while some people are rich, many others live in poverty.

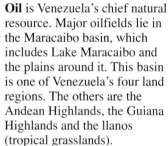

## VENEZUELA

**Area:** 912,050sq km (352,145sq miles)
**Highest point:** Pico Bolívar 5,002m (16,411ft)
**Population:** 25,730,000
**Capital and largest city:** Caracas
(pop 3,226,000)
**Other large cities:**
Maracaibo (1,901,000)
Valencia (1,893,000)
**Official language:** Spanish
**Religion:** Christianity (Roman Catholic 92%)
**Government:** Federal republic
**Currency:** Bolívar

**Oil** is Venezuela's chief natural resource. Major oilfields lie in the Maracaibo basin, which includes Lake Maracaibo and the plains around it. This basin is one of Venezuela's four land regions. The others are the Andean Highlands, the Guiana Highlands and the llanos (tropical grasslands).

**Butterflies** are common in the rainforests and grasslands of Venezuela. The country's wildlife includes pumas, jaguars, monkeys, sloths, anteaters, crocodiles and snakes, including the huge anaconda.

**Caracas**, Venezuela's capital, founded in 1567, was the birthplace of the South American hero Simón Bolívar. Caracas is a modern city, but it has slums on the outskirts. The city lies about 11km (7miles) from its port, La Guaira, on the coast.

*Caribbean Sea*

Aves · Los Roques · Orchila

*Margarita*

*La Tortuga* · Porlamar

La Guaira

**Caracas**

Maracay

**Carúpano**

**Cumaná**

an Juan de s Morros

**Barcelona** · Caripito

*ATLANTIC OCEAN*

Zaraza

**Maturin**

Calabozo

Tucupita

**El Tigre**

**Ciudad Guayana**

San Fernando de Apure

**Ciudad Bolívar** · Upata

— *Guri Dam*

*Orinoco*

El Callao

# V E N E Z U E L A

*Caura*

*Caroni*

*Angel Falls*

Puerto Ayacucho

*Guiana Highlands*

Roraima ▲ 2772m

miles
0 _____ 100
0 _____ 100
kilometres

*Orinoco*

**Tourism** is a growing industry. Venezuela has many beautiful beaches along the dry, warm Caribbean coast. Among many offshore islands is Margarita, which is noted for its pearls. Hundreds of thousands of tourists visit Venezuela every year.

**Gold and diamonds** are mined in Venezuela, together with coal, bauxite (aluminium ore), iron ore, gypsum and phosphate rock, which is used to make fertilizers. But oil and oil products make up three-quarters of the country's exports.

**Roraima** is a vast flat-topped mountain in the Guiana Highlands. It reaches 2,772m (9,904ft) at the point where the borders of Venezuela, Guyana and Brazil meet. Many fast-flowing rivers rise in these highlands.

# THE GUIANAS

Guyana (formerly British Guiana), Surinam (formerly Dutch Guiana) and French Guiana, a French overseas department, are situated in northeastern South America. Together, they are called 'the Guianas'. They have narrow coastal plains where most of the people live, with plateaus and mountains inland. Guyana is a poor country, but Surinam is more prosperous, because of its large bauxite deposits. French Guiana depends largely on financial and administrative support from France.

## GUYANA

**Area:** 214,969sq km (830,000sq miles)
**Population:** 767,000
**Capital:** Georgetown (pop 231,000)
**Official language:** English
**Religions:** Christianity 50%, Hinduism 35%, Islam 10%
**Government:** Republic
**Currency:** Guyanese dollar

## SURINAM

**Area:** 163,265sq km (63,037sq miles)
**Population:** 439,000
**Capital:** Paramaribo (pop 253,000)
**Official language:** Dutch
**Religions:** Christianity 48%, Hinduism 27%, Islam 20%
**Government:** Republic
**Currency:** Surinam dollar

## FRENCH GUIANA

**Area:** 90,000sq km (34,749sq miles)
**Population:** 200,000
**Capital:** Cayenne (pop 51,000)
**Official language:** French
**Religion:** Christianity 84%
**Government:** French overseas department
**Currency:** Euro

**Hardwoods** are important products in the Guianas. Rainforests containing valuable trees, such as greenheart, cover 90 per cent of French Guiana and Surinam and 85 per cent of Guyana. The timber industry produces logs and plywood.

**Bauxite** is the ore from which the metal aluminium is made. Bauxite and aluminium make up about half of the exports of Surinam. Guyana also exports bauxite. French Guiana has some bauxite deposits, but they are largely undeveloped.

**Georgetown**, the capital of Guyana, is built on low coastal land. Strong sea walls and drainage canals prevent flooding of the coastal plain. Only about one-third of the Guyanese live in towns, the rest are farmers.

ATLANTIC OCEAN

**Macaws**, parrots and other colourful birds live in the rainforests and savanna regions of the Guianas. Among the many animals found in the three countries are caimans, deer, monkeys, ocelots and tapirs.

**Paramaribo**

Groningen

Moengo

Kourou

Cayenne

*Coppename*

*Lake Blommestein*

*Marowijne*

*Mana*

**FRENCH GUIANA (France)**

*Approuague*

St Georges

**SURINAM**

*Julianatop*
▲ 1230m

• Saül

*Tapanahoni*

• Ouaqui

**Sugar cane** is one of the main crops of the Guianas. It makes up about a quarter of the exports of Guyana. The other major crop is rice, which is grown on about three-quarters of the farmland in Surinam. Fishing is another important industry.

**Kourou**, northwest of Cayenne, the capital of French Guiana, has been the rocket-launching site of the European Space Agency since 1968. France earns money by launching the satellites of other countries.

# BRAZIL

Brazil is the fifth largest country in the world. Only Russia, Canada, China and the United States are bigger. The country's main regions are the Amazon basin, the dry northeast, where farmers rear cattle, and the southeast, Brazil's most thickly populated region. Until 1822 the country was a Portuguese colony. Today Brazil is a rapidly developing country, but many people are poor. Farming employs 20 per cent of the people and Brazil is one of the world's leading producers of crops and livestock.

## BRAZIL

**Area** v 8,547,403sq km (3,300,156sq miles)
**Highest point:** Pico da Neblina 3,014m (9,888ft)
**Population:** 188,000,000
**Capital:** Brasília (pop, 3,099,000 )
**Largest cities:** São Paulo (17,099,000)
Rio de Janeiro (10,803,000)
Belo Horizonte (4,659,000)
Salvador (2,810,000)
**Official language:** Portuguese
**Religions:** Christianity (Roman Catholic 74%, Protestant 15%), other 5%
**Government:** Federal republic
**Currency:** Real

**Poisonous frogs** and various plants contain chemical substances used by the Amazon people for hunting and also as medicines. Curare, a drug used in anaesthetics, comes from the Amazon. Other useful substances, as yet undiscovered, may also exist in the rainforest.

**Native Americans** live in decreasing numbers in the vast rainforests of the Amazon basin. Many have given up their traditional way of life and now work in mines. The future of these people is threatened because their forest home is being destroyed. Some groups have already died out.

**Cars**, aircraft, chemicals, processed food, iron and steel, paper and textiles are leading manufactures in Brazil. The country's rich mineral reserves include bauxite, chrome, diamonds, gold, iron ore, manganese and tin.

**Amazon basin** The world's second longest river after the Nile, the Amazon has more water than any other. The Amazon basin contains the world's largest rainforest. In recent years, about a fifth of the forest has been destroyed. Plants and animals are vanishing before scientists have had a chance to study them.

Calçoene

Macapá

Marajo Island

Belém

São Luís

Parnaíba

Fortaleza

Teresina

Natal

Juàzeiro do Norte

Recife

São Francisco

Maceió

Aracaju

**BRAZIL**

Xingu

Araguaia

Tocantins

Salvador

Brasília

ATLANTIC OCEAN

Goiânia

Montes Claros

Uberaba

Belo Horizonte

Vitória

miles

0           400

0         400
kilometres

Paraná

Ribeirão Prêto

Campinas

Maringá

Ponta Grossa

São Paulo

Rio de Janeiro

Curitiba

asso Fundo

Florianópolis

Caxias do Sul

nta ria

Pôrto Alegre

Rio Grande

**Sloths** are strange hairy mammals that live in the forests. They use their hook-like claws to hang upside down from branches and rarely move except to reach more of the leaves on which they continuously feed. They remain so still that lichens and mosses grow on their fur.

**Sugar Loaf Mountain** is a landmark of Rio de Janeiro, Brazil's second largest city. The city has magnificent scenery and is famous for its beaches, nightlife and colourful carnivals. The statue of Christ the Redeemer that overlooks the city is 38m (125ft) high.

# COLOMBIA

Colombia, in the northwest corner of the continent, is South America's fourth largest country. In the north, it faces the Caribbean Sea, an arm of the Atlantic Ocean. The Pacific Ocean lies to the west. Colombia has three main regions, including the northern part of the Andes Mountains. Coastal plains lie to the north and west. The southeast contains forested plains, which are drained by tributaries of the Orinoco and Amazon rivers.

The country was the heart of the Spanish colony of New Granada, which also included Venezuela, Ecuador and Panama in Central America. It was liberated in 1819.

## COLOMBIA

**Area:** 1,138,914sq km (439,737sq miles)
**Highest point:** Cristóbal Colón 5,775m (18,947ft)
**Population:** 43,593,000
**Capital and largest city:** Bogotá (pop 7,290,000)
**Other large cities:** Medellín (2,866,000)
Cali (2,233,000)
Barranquilla (1,683,000)
**Official language:** Spanish
**Religions:** Christianity (Roman Catholic 90%), other 5%
**Government:** Republic
**Currency:** Colombian Peso

**Statues** and other carvings were made by the Chibcha people who founded a major civilization in the Andes region. A Spanish force conquered the Chibcha between 1536 and 1538. Spain introduced Roman Catholicism and ruled the country until 1819, when Simón Bolívar's army defeated Spanish forces in battle.

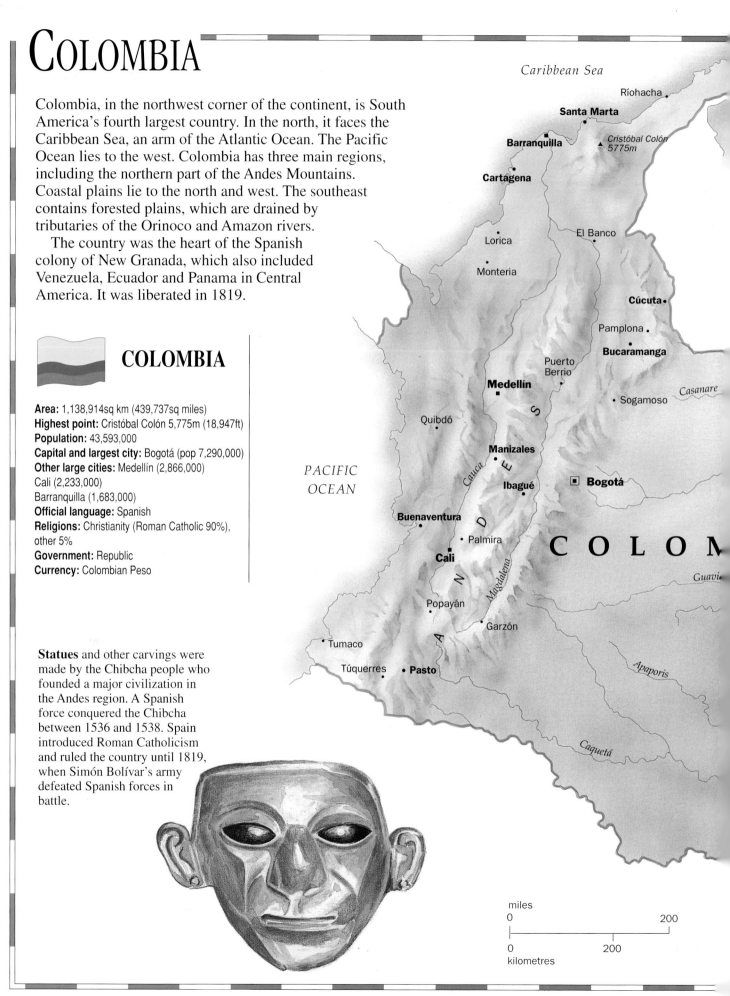

Caribbean Sea

Ríohacha

Santa Marta

Barranquilla

Cristóbal Colón 5775m

Cartagena

Lorica

El Banco

Monteria

Cúcuta

Pamplona

Bucaramanga

Puerto Berrio

Medellín

Casanare

Quibdó

Sogamoso

Manizales

Cauca

PACIFIC OCEAN

Ibagué

Bogotá

Buenaventura

Palmira

C O L O N

Cali

Magdalena

Guavi

Popayán

Garzón

Tumaco

Apaporis

Túquerres

Pasto

Caquetá

miles
0          200

0     200
kilometres

**Coffee** is Colombia's leading export crop. Other exports include oil, chemicals, wood and fish products, textiles and coal. Agriculture employs more than 20 per cent of the people. Cattle are raised and crops include bananas, cotton, rice and sugar cane.

**Bogotá**, capital of Colombia, stands on a high plateau surrounded by mountains in the eastern Andes. The Spanish conquerors of the Chibcha founded the city in 1538. The Andes region is the home of about three-quarters of the population of Colombia.

**Coca** is a native plant of Colombia. The leaves of some types of coca are used to make cocaine, a drug that is illegally exported to the United States and other countries. The cocaine trade brings wealth to the drug dealers but only violence and hardship to the poorer people.

**Jaguars** once lived all over South America. Now they are found only in the most isolated areas of forest and in national parks. They are the largest of the wild cats found in the Americas but overhunting and deforestation threaten their survival.

**Emeralds** were once traded by the Chibcha people. Today, Colombia produces more than 30 per cent of the world's emeralds. Colombia also mines coal, gold, oil and natural gas, and salt, which is used in the country's large chemical industry.

Meta

Puerto Carreño

Orinoco

Inirida

B I A

utumayo

Leticia

# ECUADOR

Ecuador lies on the equator and its name comes from the Spanish word meaning 'equator'. The country's main regions are the hot coastal lowlands, the Andes Mountains, and the humid eastern plains which are drained by the Amazon and its tributaries.

The Incas conquered the region that is now Ecuador in the late 15th century. But after the Spanish defeat of the Incas the area came under Spanish rule in 1534. Ecuador became independent in 1822.

**Marine iguanas**, giant tortoises and other unique animals live on Ecuador's Galapagos Islands, which lie about 1,000km (1,600miles) off the coast. The naturalist Charles Darwin studied the islands' animals and plants and used his discoveries in developing his theory of evolution.

 **ECUADOR**

**Area:** 283,561sq km (109,484sq miles)
**Highest point:** Chimborazo 6,267m (20,561ft)
**Population:** 13,548,000
**Capital:** Quito (pop 1,451,000)
**Largest city:** Guayaquil (2,077,000)
**Other large cities:** Cuenca (276,000) Santo Domingo (200,000)
**Official language:** Spanish
**Religions:** Christianity (Roman Catholic 90%), other 5%
**Government:** Republic
**Currency:** US dollar

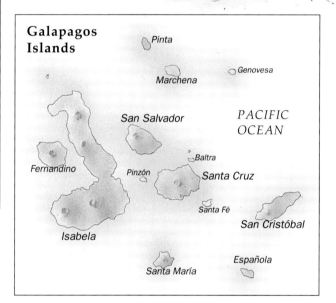

**Galapagos Islands**

Pinta
Marchena
Genovesa
San Salvador
Fernandino
Pinzón
Baltra
Santa Cruz
Santa Fé
Isabela
Santa María
San Cristóbal
Española
*PACIFIC OCEAN*

Bahía de Caráquez
Manta
Portoviejo •
Jipijapa •

*PACIFIC OCEAN*

**Fishing** is an important industry in the coastal waters, where herring and mackerel are caught. Shrimps are another important seafood and are increasingly farmed in ponds.

**Cotopaxi**, south of the capital city Quito, is one of the world's highest active volcanoes at 5,897m (19,347ft). When it erupted in 1877, avalanches of mud, caused by melting snow mixing with volcanic ash, buried large areas. Around 1,000 people were killed. Ecuador has more than 30 active volcanoes.

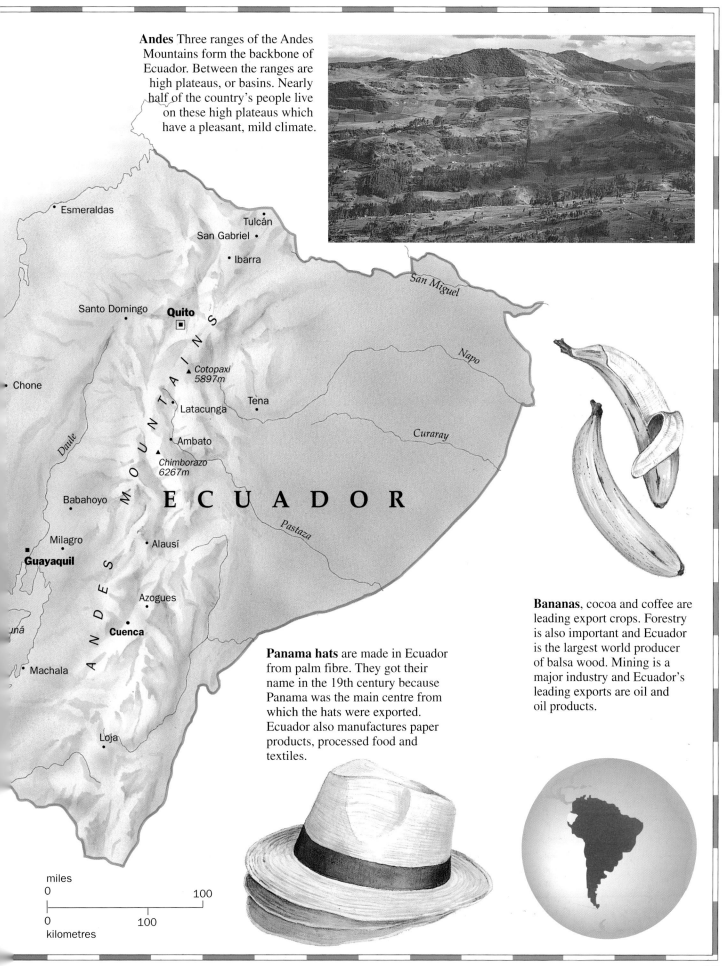

**Andes** Three ranges of the Andes Mountains form the backbone of Ecuador. Between the ranges are high plateaus, or basins. Nearly half of the country's people live on these high plateaus which have a pleasant, mild climate.

Esmeraldas

Tulcán

San Gabriel

Ibarra

San Miguel

Santo Domingo

**Quito**

Napo

Chone

▲ Cotopaxi 5897m

Tena

Latacunga

Curaray

Ambato

▲ Chimborazo 6267m

**E C U A D O R**

Daule

Babahoyo

Pastaza

Milagro

Alausí

**Guayaquil**

M O U N T A I N S

Azogues

**Cuenca**

A N D E S

Machala

Loja

miles

0                100

0      100

kilometres

**Bananas**, cocoa and coffee are leading export crops. Forestry is also important and Ecuador is the largest world producer of balsa wood. Mining is a major industry and Ecuador's leading exports are oil and oil products.

**Panama hats** are made in Ecuador from palm fibre. They got their name in the 19th century because Panama was the main centre from which the hats were exported. Ecuador also manufactures paper products, processed food and textiles.

# PERU

Behind the narrow, dry coastal plain of Peru lie the Andes Mountains, which contain active volcanoes and high plateaus between the ranges. East of the Andes are plains covered by rainforests. From about AD 1200, Peru was the heart of the great Inca civilization. Spanish soldiers conquered Peru in the 1520s and finally conquered the Incas in 1533. Peru became independent from Spain in 1821. Native Americans now make up nearly half of the people and the Inca language, Quechua, is one of Peru's two official languages.

## PERU

**Area:** 1,285,216sq km (496,225sq miles)
**Highest point:** Huarascarán 6,768m (22,205ft)
**Population:** 28,303,000
**Capital and largest city:** Lima (pop 7,899,000)
**Other large cities:** Arequipa (710,000)
Callao (424,000)
**Official languages:** Spanish, Quechua
**Religion:** Christianity (Roman Catholic 80%)
**Government:** Republic
**Currency:** Nuevo sol

**Toucans** are tropical birds of Central and South America. There are many different kinds, all with large, brightly-coloured bills. Some are found in Peru's eastern forests, where they gather in small flocks high in the trees.

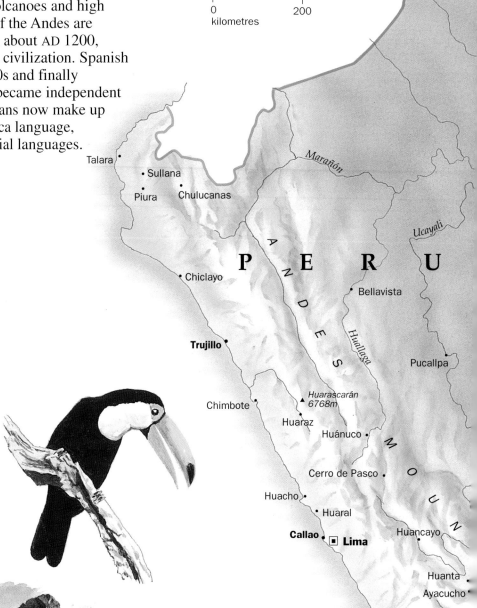

**Machu Picchu**, an ancient Inca city, stands on a peak in south-central Peru. The Incas ruled one of the largest Native American empires. At its height, the empire stretched from southern Colombia, through Ecuador and Peru, into Chile and Argentina.

**Lima**, Peru's capital, lies just inland from its port of Callao. It is Peru's chief industrial city, but manufacturing is small-scale. Farming is the main occupation and mining is also important. Copper is the country's chief export. Peru also produces oil, silver, zinc and other minerals.

**Huge patterns** and drawings of animals are marked on the desert floor at Nazca, in southern Peru. Some are 2km (1.2miles) long and completely visible only from the air. Nobody knows the significance of these ancient markings or who made them, but archaeologists think they may have had a religious or astronomical purpose.

**Source of the Amazon** The mighty River Amazon rises in the Peruvian Andes in a small stream called the Apurimac. The Apurimac eventually flows into the River Ucayali, which flows north to join the River Marañón. From here the Amazon flows east to the Atlantic Ocean.

**Lake Titicaca**, the world's highest navigable lake, lies on Peru's border with Bolivia. It occupies a basin between ranges of the Andes Mountains, at 3,812m (12,507ft) above sea level. Local people use reed boats to sail on the lake.

Iquitos

Amazon

Urubamba

Machu
Picchu

Cuzco

Apurimac

N
D
E
S

Juliaca

Puno

Lake
Titicaca

Arequipa

Mollendo

Tacna

Puerto
Maldonado

# BOLIVIA

Bolivia is a landlocked country and one of the poorest in South America. It contains part of the Andes Mountains, together with forested plains in the north and east. Native Americans have lived in the area for around 10,000 years. The main groups today are the Aymara and the Quechua. Their languages are both official, together with Spanish. Bolivian culture, like that of much of South America, is a mix of local and European influences.

## BOLIVIA

**Area:** 1,098,581sq km (424,165sq miles)
**Highest point:** Nevado Sajama 6,542m (21,463ft)
**Population:** 8,989,000
**Capital and largest city:** La Paz (pop 1,477,000)
**Judicial capital:** Sucre (212,000)
**Other large cities:** Santa Cruz (1,016,000)
Cochabamba (966,000)
**Official languages:** Spanish, Aymara, Quechua
**Religion:** Christianity (Roman Catholic 95%)
**Government:** Republic
**Currency:** Boliviano

**Potatoes** and wheat are grown on the Altiplano, a plateau between the eastern and western ranges of the Andes. Bananas, cocoa, coffee and maize are grown at lower, warmer levels. Agriculture employs almost a half of Bolivia's people.

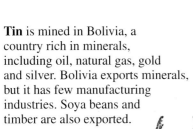

**Tin** is mined in Bolivia, a country rich in minerals, including oil, natural gas, gold and silver. Bolivia exports minerals, but it has few manufacturing industries. Soya beans and timber are also exported.

miles
0 — 100

0 — 100
kilometres

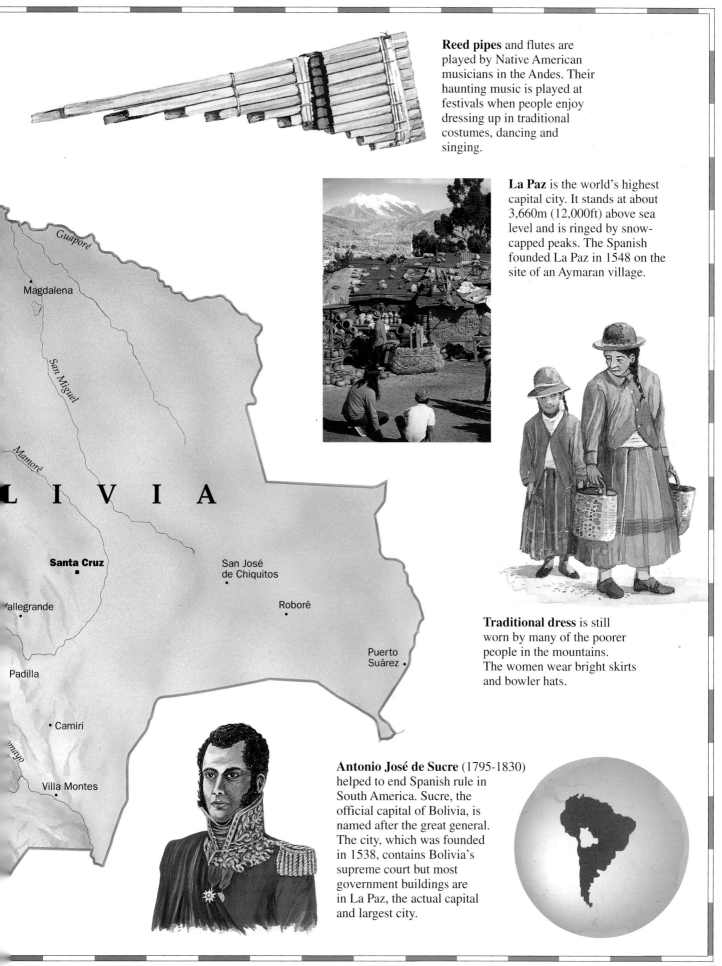

**Reed pipes** and flutes are played by Native American musicians in the Andes. Their haunting music is played at festivals when people enjoy dressing up in traditional costumes, dancing and singing.

**La Paz** is the world's highest capital city. It stands at about 3,660m (12,000ft) above sea level and is ringed by snow-capped peaks. The Spanish founded La Paz in 1548 on the site of an Aymaran village.

Guaporé

Magdalena

San Miguel

Mamoré

L I V I A

Santa Cruz

San José
de Chiquitos

Roboré

Vallegrande

Puerto
Suárez

Padilla

**Traditional dress** is still worn by many of the poorer people in the mountains. The women wear bright skirts and bowler hats.

Camiri

mayo

Villa Montes

**Antonio José de Sucre** (1795-1830) helped to end Spanish rule in South America. Sucre, the official capital of Bolivia, is named after the great general. The city, which was founded in 1538, contains Bolivia's supreme court but most government buildings are in La Paz, the actual capital and largest city.

# PARAGUAY

Paraguay is a landlocked country. Rivers make up most of its boundaries. The land consists mostly of large plains, plateaus and hills. The climate is warm and humid. Most people live in the east. Paraguay's earliest-known people were Native Americans called the Guaraní. The Guaraní language is now one of the country's two official languages. Most of the people in Paraguay are mestizos, of mixed Native American and European origin.

## PARAGUAY

**Area:** 406,752sq km (150,048sq miles)
**Highest point:** 680m (2,231ft), in the southeast
**Population:** 6,506,000
**Capital and largest city:** Asunción (pop1,639,000)
**Other large cities:** Ciudad del Este (287,000) San Lorenzo (245,000)
**Official languages:** Spanish, Guaraní
**Religion:** Christianity (Roman Catholic 90%)
**Government:** Republic
**Currency:** Guaraní

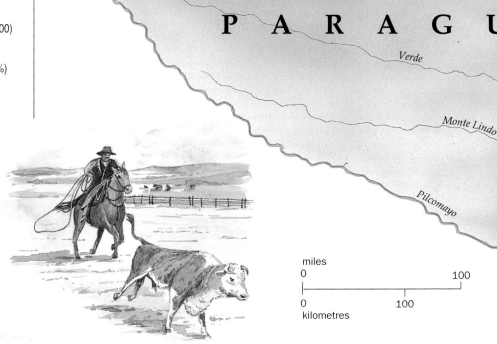

**Gauchos** are cowboys who work on ranches in Paraguay and elsewhere on the grassy plains called pampas. Farming employs about a third of Paraguay's people. Soya bean flour, cotton, oilseed cakes, vegetable oils, meat and hides are leading exports.

**Hydroelectric power stations** provide Paraguay with abundant electricity. Paraguay shares the huge Itaipú Dam with Brazil. When it was completed in 1991, this dam became one of the world's largest.

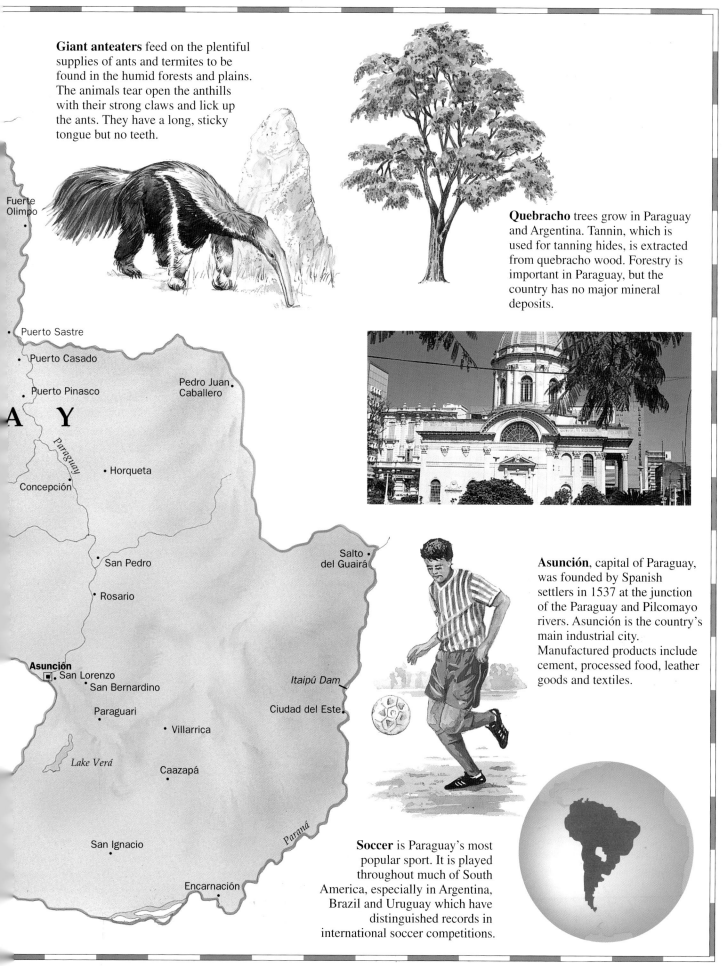

**Giant anteaters** feed on the plentiful supplies of ants and termites to be found in the humid forests and plains. The animals tear open the anthills with their strong claws and lick up the ants. They have a long, sticky tongue but no teeth.

**Quebracho** trees grow in Paraguay and Argentina. Tannin, which is used for tanning hides, is extracted from quebracho wood. Forestry is important in Paraguay, but the country has no major mineral deposits.

**Asunción**, capital of Paraguay, was founded by Spanish settlers in 1537 at the junction of the Paraguay and Pilcomayo rivers. Asunción is the country's main industrial city. Manufactured products include cement, processed food, leather goods and textiles.

**Soccer** is Paraguay's most popular sport. It is played throughout much of South America, especially in Argentina, Brazil and Uruguay which have distinguished records in international soccer competitions.

Fuerte Olimpo

Puerto Sastre

Puerto Casado

Puerto Pinasco

Pedro Juan Caballero

A Y

*Paraguay*

Horqueta

Concepción

San Pedro

Salto del Guairá

Rosario

Asunción
San Lorenzo
San Bernardino

*Itaipú Dam*

Ciudad del Este

Paraguari

Villarrica

*Lake Verá*

Caazapá

*Paraná*

San Ignacio

Encarnación

21

# CHILE

Chile has an unusual shape. It is more than ten times as long as it is wide. Its eastern borders run through the high Andes Mountains. To the west the land descends through valleys and basins to the coastal plain along the Pacific Ocean. In the north is the bleak Atacama Desert. In the centre is the Central Valley, which has hot, dry summers and mild, rainy winters. This region contains three-quarters of the population. To the south, it gets colder and rainier. The far south is one of the world's stormiest places.

Mestizos make up about 70 per cent of Chile's population and people of European descent 20 per cent. Native Americans make up only 5 per cent of the population. Until 1818 most of the country was colonized by Spain.

## CHILE

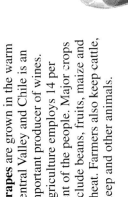

**Area:** 756,626sq km (292,135sq miles)
**Highest point:** Ojos del Salado 6,880m (22,572ft)
**Population:** 16,134,000
**Capital and largest city:** Santiago (pop 5,478,000)
**Other large cities:** Antofagasta (319,000)
Viña del Mar (300,000)
Valparaíso (287,000)
Concepción (217,000)
**Official language:** Spanish
**Religion:** Christianity (Roman Catholic 89%)
**Government:** Republic
**Currency:** Chilean peso

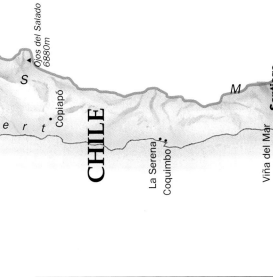

*PACIFIC OCEAN*

**Atacama Desert** This desert is one of the driest in the world. It stretches about 1,700km (1,056miles) south from the Peruvian border. The region has rich deposits of copper and of sodium nitrate, which is used to make explosives and fertilizers.

**Grapes** are grown in the warm Central Valley and Chile is an important producer of wines. Agriculture employs 14 per cent of the people. Major crops include beans, fruits, maize and wheat. Farmers also keep cattle, sheep and other animals.

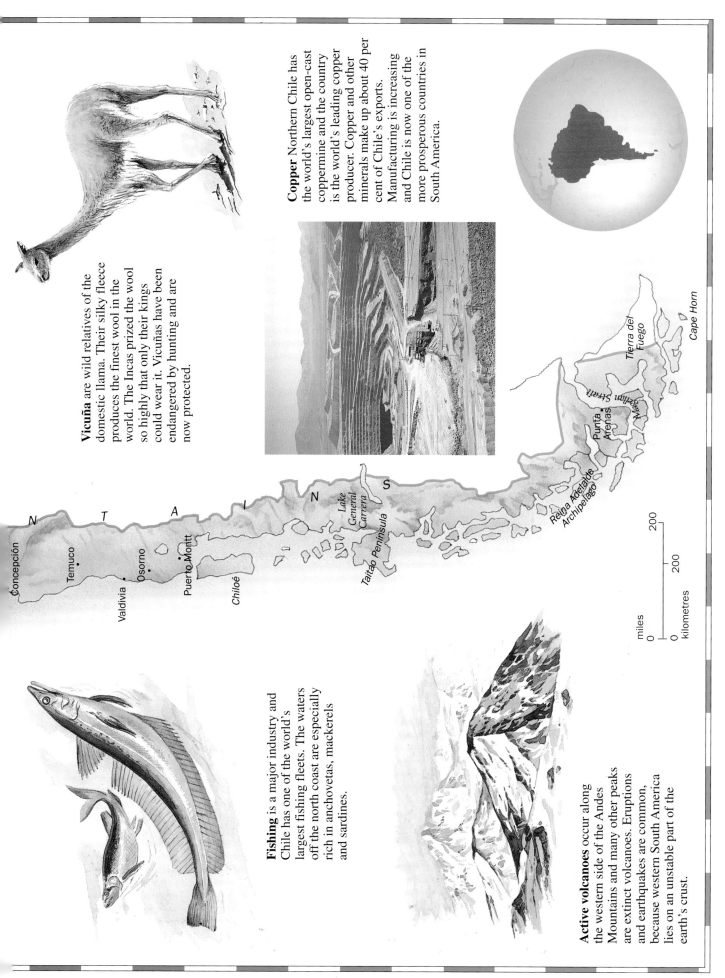

**Vicuña** are wild relatives of the domestic llama. Their silky fleece produces the finest wool in the world. The Incas prized the wool so highly that only their kings could wear it. Vicuñas have been endangered by hunting and are now protected.

**Copper** Northern Chile has the world's largest open-cast coppermine and the country is the world's leading copper producer. Copper and other minerals make up about 40 per cent of Chile's exports. Manufacturing is increasing and Chile is now one of the more prosperous countries in South America.

**Fishing** is a major industry and Chile has one of the world's largest fishing fleets. The waters off the north coast are especially rich in anchovetas, mackerels and sardines.

**Active volcanoes** occur along the western side of the Andes Mountains and many other peaks are extinct volcanoes. Eruptions and earthquakes are common, because western South America lies on an unstable part of the earth's crust.

Concepción
Temuco
Valdivia
Osorno
Puerto Montt
Chiloé
Lake General Carrera
Taitao Peninsula
Reina Adelaide Archipelago
Punta Arenas
Magellan Strait
Tierra del Fuego
Cape Horn

N  T  A  I  N  S

miles
0        200
kilometres
0        200

23

# ARGENTINA

Argentina is the second largest country in South America. The Andes Mountains lie in the west. In the centre and north lie large plains, with the fertile pampas region in east-central Argentina around the capital Buenos Aires. In the south, the Andes overlook a plateau region called Patagonia. At the tip of Argentina lies the island of Tierra del Fuego, separated from the mainland by the Magellan Strait which links the Atlantic and Pacific oceans. The weather is warm and wet in the north and cold and dry in the south.

Until 1816 Argentina was part of a Spanish colony. About 85 per cent of the people are of European descent. Mestizos make up most of the remaining 15 per cent.

## ARGENTINA

**Area:** 2,780,400sq km (1,073,519sq miles)
**Highest point:** Aconcagua 6,960m (22,835ft)
**Population:** 39,922,000
**Capital and largest city:** Buenos Aires (pop 13,047,000)
**Other large cities:** Córdoba (2,866,000) Rosario (1,231,000)
**Official language:** Spanish
**Religion:** Christianity (Roman Catholic 91%)
**Government:** Republic
**Currency:** Argentine peso

**Iguaçu Falls** These magnificent falls lie on the River Iguaçu on the Argentina-Brazil border. The falls are about 4km (22miles) wide and up to 82m (269ft) high.

**Aconcagua**, an extinct volcano in the Andes close to the border with Chile, is the highest peak in North and South America. It reaches a height of 6,960m (22,835ft) above sea level.

Iguaçu Falls

Paraná

Uruguay

Paraguay

Pilcomayo

*G r a n   C h a c o*

Posadas

Corrientes

Resistencia

Goya

Santa Fe

Paraná

Concordia

Tartagal

San Salvador

Salta

**San Miguel de Tucumán**

Catamarca

**Córdoba**

Rio Cuarto

San Juan

*Aconcagua 6960m* ▲ **Mendoza** Godoy Cruz

San Rafael

Junin

San Isidro

Avellaneda

**Buenos Aires** **La Plata**

*Rio del Plata*

Paraná

**Rosario**

*P a m p a s*

A R G E N T I N A

S   N   I   A   T   N   U   O   M

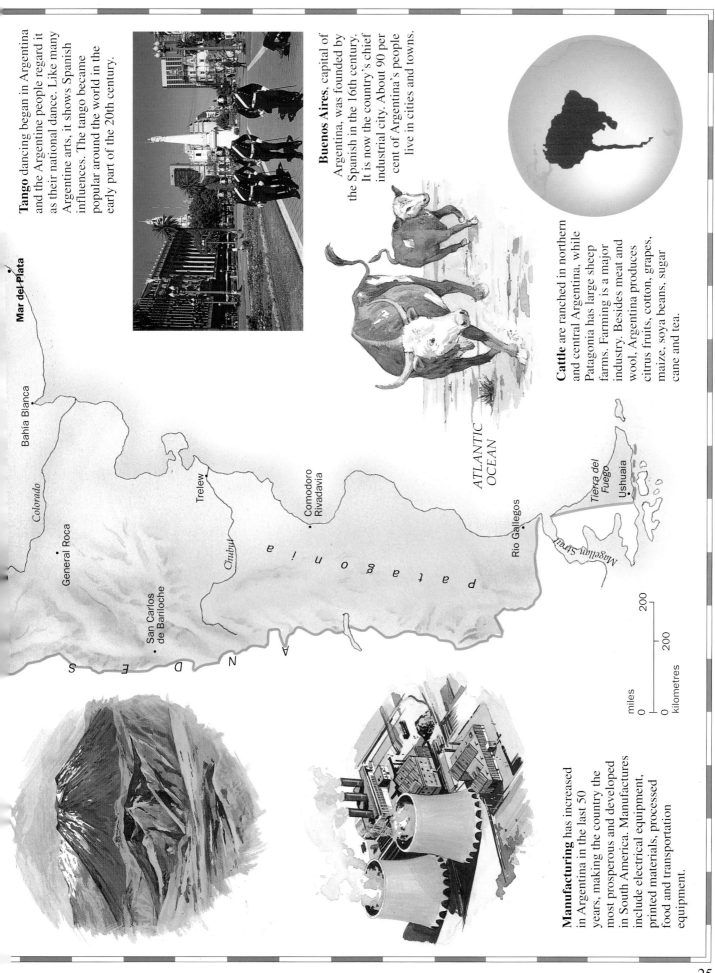

**Tango** dancing began in Argentina and the Argentine people regard it as their national dance. Like many Argentine arts, it shows Spanish influences. The tango became popular around the world in the early part of the 20th century.

**Buenos Aires**, capital of Argentina, was founded by the Spanish in the 16th century. It is now the country's chief industrial city. About 90 per cent of Argentina's people live in cities and towns.

**Cattle** are ranched in northern and central Argentina, while Patagonia has large sheep farms. Farming is a major industry. Besides meat and wool, Argentina produces citrus fruits, cotton, grapes, maize, soya beans, sugar cane and tea.

**Manufacturing** has increased in Argentina in the last 50 years, making the country the most prosperous and developed in South America. Manufactures include electrical equipment, printed materials, processed food and transportation equipment.

Mar del-Plata

Bahía Blanca

Colorado

General Roca

San Carlos de Bariloche

Trelew

Chubut

Comodoro Rivadavia

A N D E S

P a t a g o n i a

Río Gallegos

Magellan Strait

Tierra del Fuego

Ushuaia

ATLANTIC OCEAN

miles
0

kilometres
0

200

200

# URUGUAY

Uruguay is South America's second smallest independent country after Surinam. It is a land of grassy plains and hills.

About 90 per cent of the people now live in cities and towns. Native Americans once occupied Uruguay, but only a few Amerindians remain. The country was part of a Spanish colony until 1828. People of European descent make up 88 per cent of the population, mestizos 8 per cent, and descendants of black Africans 4 per cent.

## URUGUAY

**Area:** 177,414sq km (68,500sq miles)
**Highest point:** Mirador Nacional 501m (1,644ft)
**Population:** 3,432,000
**Capital and largest city:** Montevideo (pop 1,341,000)
**Other largest cities:** Salto (101,000) Paysandú (73,000)
**Official language:** Spanish
**Religion:** Christianity (Roman Catholic 66%)
**Government:** Republic
**Currency:** Uruguayan peso

**Textiles** are among the leading manufactures produced in Uruguay. Other manufactures include beer, cement and processed food. Uruguay is one of the more prosperous of the developing countries in South America.

**Livestock farming** is the most valuable form of agriculture in Uruguay. Sheep and cattle ranches make up four-fifths of the land. Major products include beef, hides and leather goods, and wool. Crops include maize, potatoes, sugar beet and wheat.

**Montevideo**, Uruguay's capital and chief port, stands on the coast where the Rio de la Plata estuary meets the Atlantic Ocean. Founded in 1726, Montevideo and its suburbs contain most of Uruguay's manufacturing industries.

Salto

Uruguay

Paysandú

Paso de los To

Negro

Fray Bentos

Mercedes

Dolores

Trinidad •

Rio de la Plata

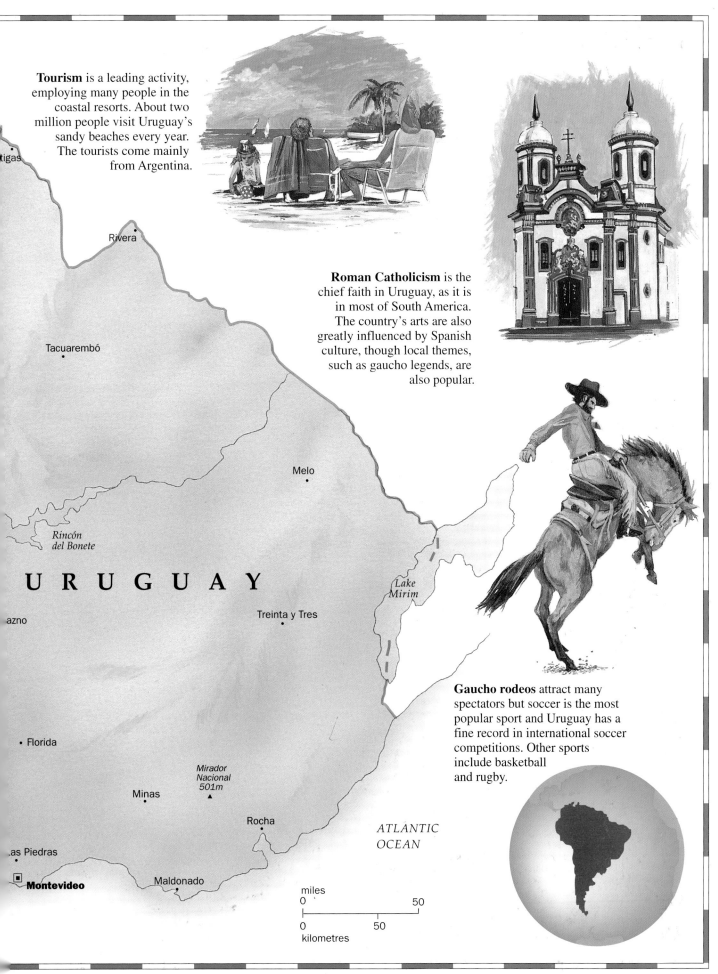

**Tourism** is a leading activity, employing many people in the coastal resorts. About two million people visit Uruguay's sandy beaches every year. The tourists come mainly from Argentina.

tigas

Rivera

**Roman Catholicism** is the chief faith in Uruguay, as it is in most of South America. The country's arts are also greatly influenced by Spanish culture, though local themes, such as gaucho legends, are also popular.

Tacuarembó

Melo

*Rincón del Bonete*

# U R U G U A Y

azno

*Lake Mirim*

Treinta y Tres

**Gaucho rodeos** attract many spectators but soccer is the most popular sport and Uruguay has a fine record in international soccer competitions. Other sports include basketball and rugby.

Florida

Mirador Nacional 501m ▲

Minas

Rocha

*ATLANTIC OCEAN*

as Piedras

■ **Montevideo**

Maldonado

miles
0        50

0        50
kilometres

# PEOPLE AND BELIEFS

South America contains between five and six per cent of the world's population. Large parts of the continent are nearly empty of people. They include the Amazon basin, the Atacama Desert and Patagonia. One densely populated region includes southeastern Brazil and northeastern Argentina. It contains the continent's largest cities: São Paulo and Rio de Janeiro in Brazil and Buenos Aires in Argentina. Parts of the high plateaus in the Andes Mountains and also central Chile are thickly populated.

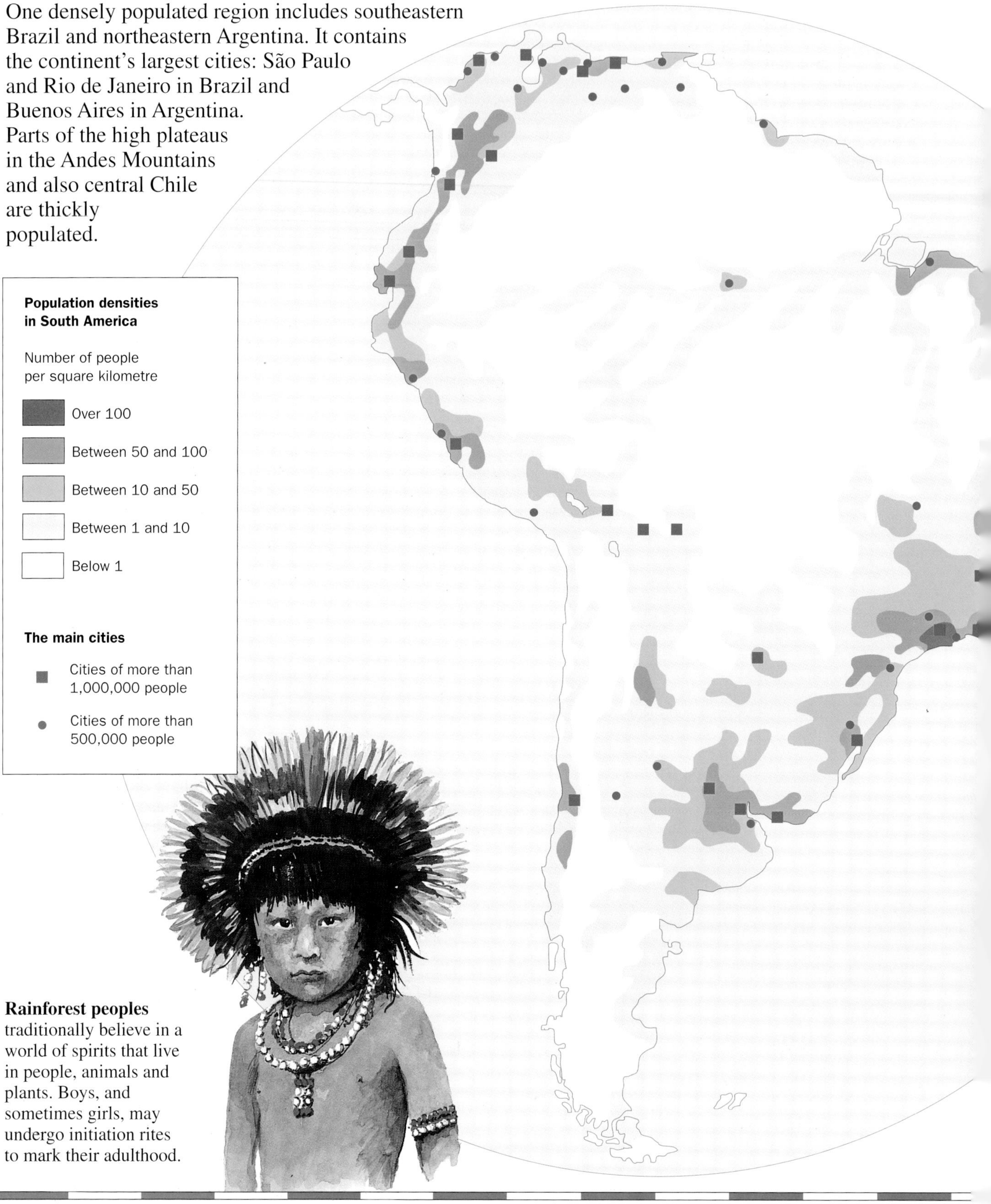

**Population densities in South America**

Number of people per square kilometre

- Over 100
- Between 50 and 100
- Between 10 and 50
- Between 1 and 10
- Below 1

**The main cities**

- Cities of more than 1,000,000 people
- Cities of more than 500,000 people

**Rainforest peoples** traditionally believe in a world of spirits that live in people, animals and plants. Boys, and sometimes girls, may undergo initiation rites to mark their adulthood.

## Population and area

Brazil, one of the world's largest countries, is larger than the entire continent of Australia. Brazil and Argentina are the two giants of South America. They make up more than three-fifths of the area of the continent and contain about three-fifths of its population. Surinam is the smallest independent country, though French Guiana is even smaller.

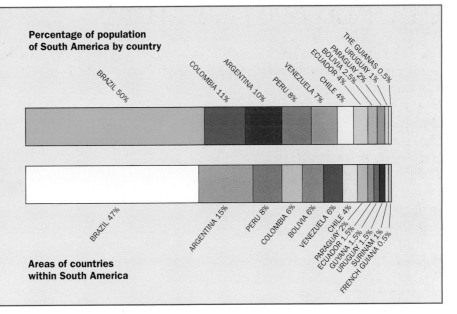

Percentage of population of South America by country

BRAZIL 50% · COLOMBIA 11% · ARGENTINA 10% · PERU 8% · VENEZUELA 7% · ECUADOR 4% · CHILE 4% · BOLIVIA 2.5% · PARAGUAY 2% · URUGUAY 1% · THE GUIANAS 0.5%

BRAZIL 47% · ARGENTINA 15% · PERU 8% · COLOMBIA 6% · BOLIVIA 6% · VENEZUELA 6% · CHILE 4% · PARAGUAY 2% · ECUADOR 1.5% · GUYANA 1.5% · URUGUAY 1.5% · SURINAM 1% · FRENCH GUIANA 0.5%

Areas of countries within South America

## South Americans and religions

The first South Americans were descended from people who migrated from the north through Central America. As they moved south, they formed many groups, each with its own language and customs.

European settlers, who began to arrive in the early 16th century, forced the Native Americans to work for them. They also imported black slaves from Africa. Millions died of harsh treatment and illnesses, such as influenza and measles, which the settlers brought with them. Only Bolivia, Peru and Ecuador still have large groups of Native Americans. Many other South Americans are mestizos, of mixed Native American and European descent.

As well as diseases, the European settlers brought with them the Christian religion. Missionaries forced the people to abandon their traditional gods and beliefs. Today most South Americans (over 90%) are Roman Catholics but an increasing number belong to Protestant churches.

## Languages

Most of the people of South America speak Spanish or - in Brazil - Portuguese. English is spoken in Guyana, Dutch in Surinam, French in French Guiana. Quechua, Aymara and Guaraní are Native American languages that have survived in Peru, Bolivia and Paraguay. Other ancient languages are also spoken by small groups of Native Americans. The survival of some of the peoples shown on the map is endangered.

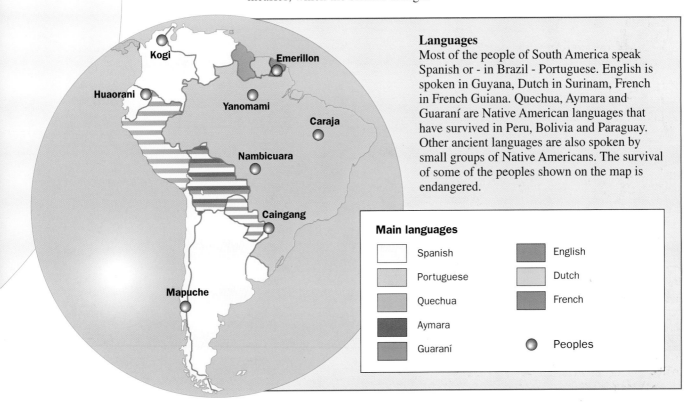

**Main languages**

- Spanish
- Portuguese
- Quechua
- Aymara
- Guaraní
- English
- Dutch
- French
- Peoples

# CLIMATE AND VEGETATION

South America extends from the steamy, hot tropical regions in the north to the cold windswept island of Tierra del Fuego in the far south.

The continent also includes the Atacama Desert, which extends along the coast of Peru and northern Chile. One of the driest places on our planet, parts of it have had no rainfall for 400 years. Patagonia, in southern Argentina, is another dry region.

In the Andes Mountains, the climate changes the higher one goes. Tropical forests grow on the lower slopes near the equator. But higher up are cold pastures overlooked by snow-capped peaks.

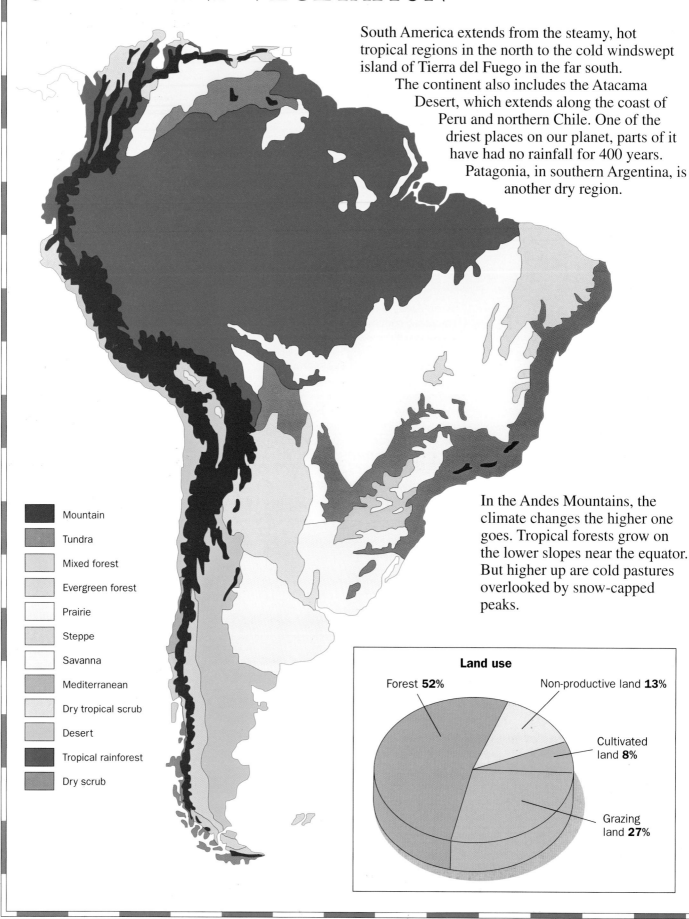

Mountain

Tundra

Mixed forest

Evergreen forest

Prairie

Steppe

Savanna

Mediterranean

Dry tropical scrub

Desert

Tropical rainforest

Dry scrub

**Land use**

Forest **52%**

Non-productive land **13%**

Cultivated land **8%**

Grazing land **27%**

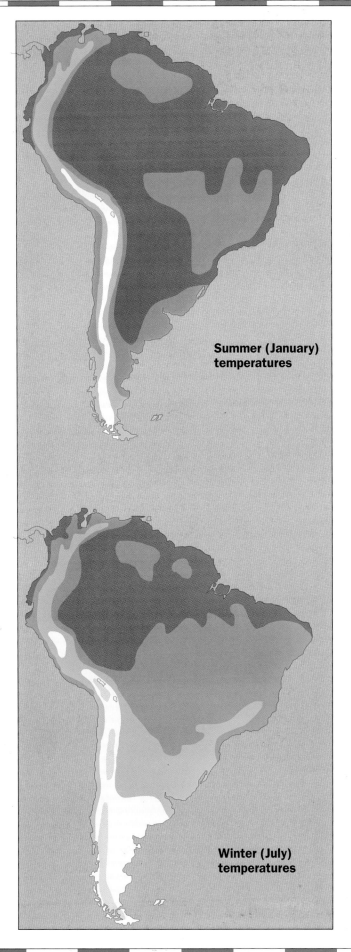

**Summer (January) temperatures**

**Winter (July) temperatures**

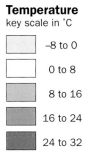

**Temperature**
key scale in °C

| | |
|---|---|
| | –8 to 0 |
| | 0 to 8 |
| | 8 to 16 |
| | 16 to 24 |
| | 24 to 32 |

### Range of climates

Most of South America has a warm climate. This is because much of the land lies in the tropics, with the equator passing through Ecuador, Colombia and Brazil. High temperatures are accompanied by high and heavy rainfall, encouraging the growth of the world's largest rainforest which covers most of equatorial South America.

In the far north, where rain occurs only in one season, the forest merges into the llanos, a grassy region with scattered trees, like the tropical savanna of Africa.

Southern South America has cooler winters than the tropical lands to the north. The grassy pampas region of northeastern Argentina and Uruguay has a mild, subtropical climate. In winter, cold winds from the Antarctic may bring cold weather and light snow to southern South America.

The pampas region, like the North American prairies, has enough rainfall to support the growth of tall grasses. But to the west, the land becomes drier and the pampas merges into dry steppe. But the driest region is the Atacama Desert, where hundreds of years may pass without any rain. Patagonia, in southern Argentina, is also dry.

**Annual rainfall**
in mm

| | |
|---|---|
| | Above 3000 |
| | 2000 - 3000 |
| | 1000 - 2000 |
| | 500 - 1000 |
| | 250 - 500 |
| | 0 - 250 |

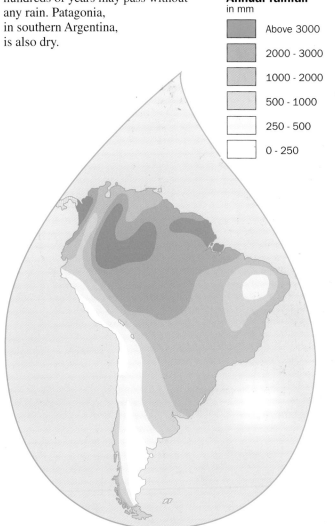

# ECOLOGY AND ENVIRONMENT

Western South America, including the high Andes Mountains, is an unstable part of the world, where frequent earthquakes and volcanic eruptions cause great damage. People also cause many problems. The rapid destruction of the Amazon rainforest is a major disaster that may upset the ecology of the whole world. In some dry areas, farmers are clearing the land. Without the protection of plants, the soil is washed away by rain or swept away by winds, leaving bare, infertile ground.

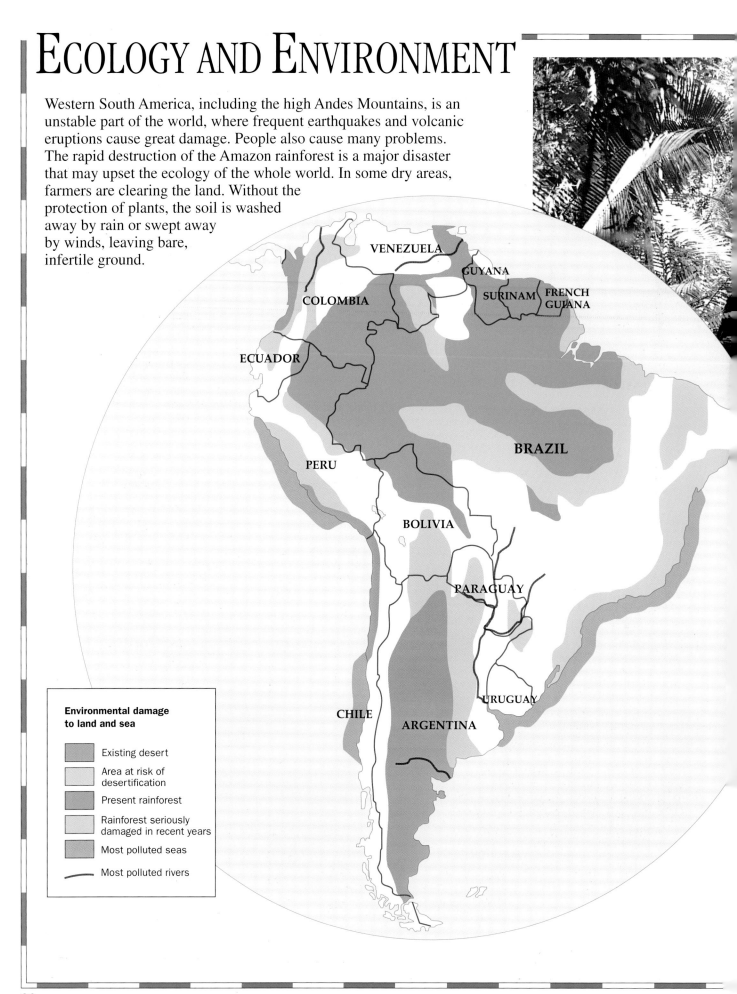

VENEZUELA

GUYANA

COLOMBIA

SURINAM

FRENCH GUIANA

ECUADOR

BRAZIL

PERU

BOLIVIA

PARAGUAY

URUGUAY

CHILE

ARGENTINA

**Environmental damage to land and sea**

Existing desert

Area at risk of desertification

Present rainforest

Rainforest seriously damaged in recent years

Most polluted seas

Most polluted rivers

The destruction of the rainforest is a global problem that requires an international solution.

## Damaging the environment

In 1995, an area of Amazon rainforest the size of Belgium was destroyed by fire. The destruction of rainforest has been increasing rapidly over the last 30 to 40 years. Some forests are cleared by loggers, who sell the wood they obtain. Other areas are cleared to create new farms and cattle ranches. But the rain soon washes out the minerals from the soil on the cleared land, which often becomes barren and useless. Forest clearance not only causes the extinction of animals and plants, it also threatens the Native Americans in the forests. Nearly 100 groups of Native Americans have been wiped out in the last century.

Pollution is caused by factories and cars in the cities, which are growing bigger and bigger as people leave rural areas in the hope of finding jobs. Many remain unemployed and homeless, scratching a living in the slums and shanty towns that have grown up around major cities. Lack of food and poor sanitation bring disease and hardship.

## Endangered species

South America's human population is increasing quickly. People need land for homes and for crops, they need wood for building and for fuel, and they need roads and transport, all of which threaten the plants and animals in large areas which were once almost empty of people. The greatest loss of species is occurring in the Amazon basin, where scientists reckon that many plant and animal species have been destroyed completely, probably including species that might have proved useful in producing medicines to cure diseases.

Farming in the pampas region of Argentina and Uruguay, as well as sheep farming in Patagonia, have led to a decline in various species, including deer. Rapid population growth in the Andes Mountains and hunting have threatened the spectacled bear and the Andean condor.

Morpho butterfly

**Some endangered species of South America**

**Mammals**
Giant otter
Jaguar
Spectacled bear
Uakari
Vicuña

**Birds**
Andean condor
Harpy eagle
Macaws (many species)

**Insects**
Morpho butterfly

**Plants**
Alerce cypress
Chilean false larch

## Natural hazards

Massive volcanoes are dotted throughout the high Andes Mountains. When they erupt, they often cover the land in hot ash. Melted snow mixes with the ash, creating mud flows. Fast-moving rivers of mud surge downwards, submerging villages and towns. Devastating earthquakes are common. They are caused by movements in the huge plates that form the earth's hard outer layers. In South America, the Nazca plate under the southeastern Pacific Ocean is sinking under the South American plate. When it moves, the land shakes. The rocks along the edge of the plate are melted, producing lava to fuel the volcanoes.

▲ Active volcanoes

◯ Earthquake zone

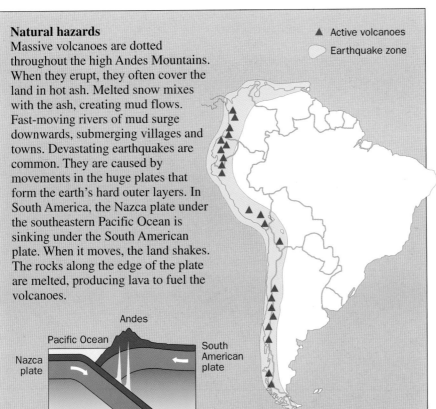

# ECONOMY

South America has many natural resources, including minerals, but many of the resources have not been developed. As a result, South America is a poorer continent than North America, Europe and Australia. The richest countries, which have developed many industries, include Argentina, Brazil and Chile. Venezuela is also fairly prosperous because of its large oil deposits. The poorest countries are Guyana and Bolivia.

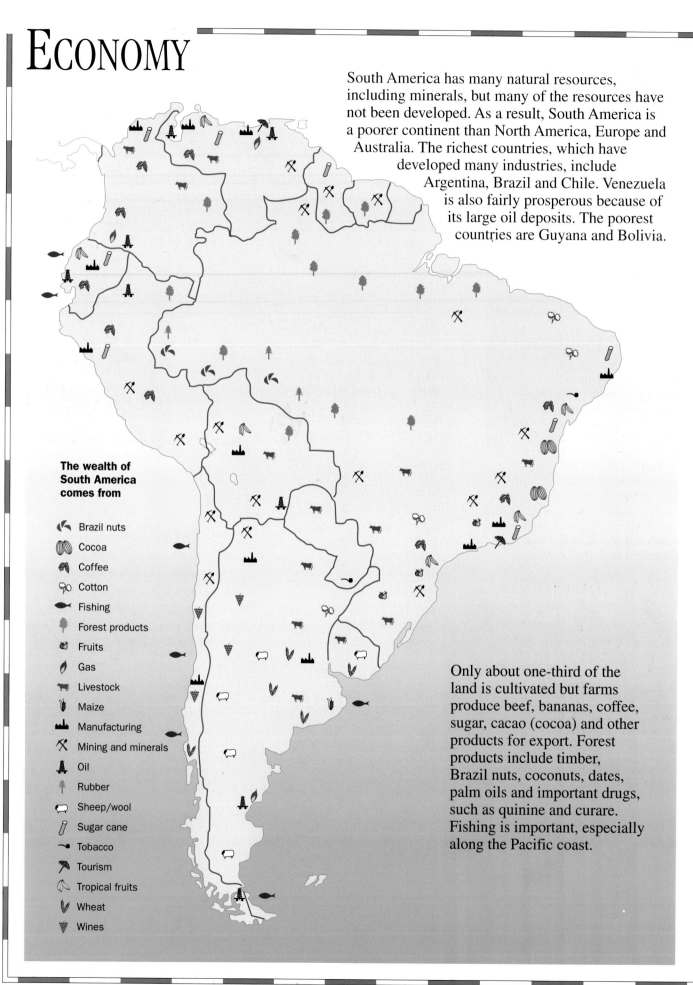

**The wealth of South America comes from**

- Brazil nuts
- Cocoa
- Coffee
- Cotton
- Fishing
- Forest products
- Fruits
- Gas
- Livestock
- Maize
- Manufacturing
- Mining and minerals
- Oil
- Rubber
- Sheep/wool
- Sugar cane
- Tobacco
- Tourism
- Tropical fruits
- Wheat
- Wines

Only about one-third of the land is cultivated but farms produce beef, bananas, coffee, sugar, cacao (cocoa) and other products for export. Forest products include timber, Brazil nuts, coconuts, dates, palm oils and important drugs, such as quinine and curare. Fishing is important, especially along the Pacific coast.

## Gross domestic product

In order to compare the economies of countries, experts work out the gross domestic product (GDP) of the countries in US dollars. The GDP is the total value of all the goods and services produced in a country in a year. The chart, right, shows that the GDP of Brazil is more than the GDPs of all the other South American countries combined. However, Brazil's total GDP is only one-tenth of the GDP of the United States. The South American countries with the lowest GDPs are Guyana and Surinam.

**GDP for the countries of South America** (in billions of dollars)

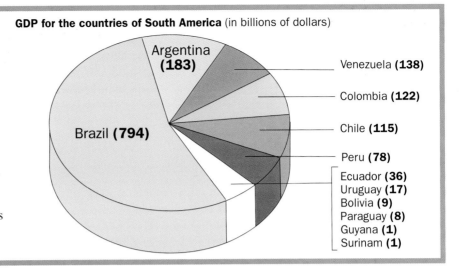

- Argentina **(183)**
- Brazil **(794)**
- Venezuela **(138)**
- Colombia **(122)**
- Chile **(115)**
- Peru **(78)**
- Ecuador **(36)**
- Uruguay **(17)**
- Bolivia **(9)**
- Paraguay **(8)**
- Guyana **(1)**
- Surinam **(1)**

## Per capita GDPs

Per capita means per head or per person. Per capita GDPs are worked out by dividng the GDP by the population. For example the per capita GDP of Argentina is US$20,000, which makes it an upper middle-income country. By contrast, Guyana is a low-income economy with a per capita GDP of only $3,400.

## Sources of energy

Venezuela is South America's leading producer of oil and it ranks among the world's top ten producers. Argentina and Brazil also produce some oil, but most South American countries have to import oil and other fuels to power their industries.

South America's rivers provide an important source of water power, which is used to produce cheap electricity. For example, most of Brazil's electricity comes from hydroelectric power plants. The Itaipú power plant on the Paraná River on the border of Brazil and Paraguay and the Guri power plant on the Caroni River in Venezuela are among the world's largest.

Brazil leads the world in production of biofuels, such as ethanol produced from sugar-cane, which is used to power motor vehicles.

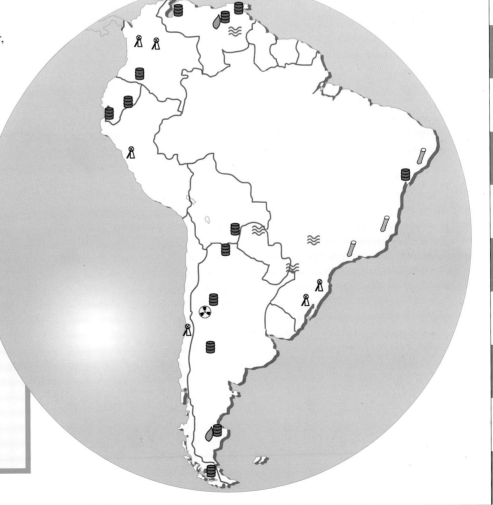

### Sources of energy found in South America

- Oil
- Gas
- Hydroelectricity
- Coal
- Uranium
- Biofuels

# POLITICS AND HISTORY

South America contains 12 independent countries. They are all republics with elected governments and have presidents as their heads of state. The other territories are French Guiana and the British Falkland Islands.

Since most of the countries of South America became independent in the early 19th century, many have suffered from instability. In the 20th century, military leaders ruled as dictators in several countries.

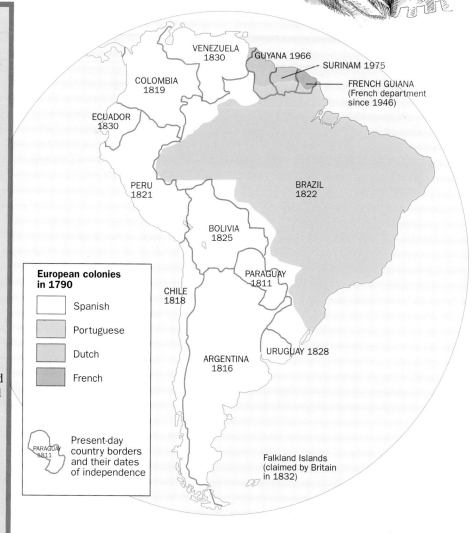

**Francisco Pizarro** (1478?-1541) who led the Spanish force that finally conquered the Incas in 1533.

### Great events

By 6000BC Native Americans had spread throughout South America. They lived as hunter-gatherers, before settling down to farm the land wherever they could. Little is known of the cultures of the ancient forest peoples, but in the Andes the great Inca civilization grew up and left remarkable remains.

Despite their great power, the Incas were defeated in 1532-3 by a Spanish force. Most of South America was soon occupied either by Spain or Portugal, which took Brazil. The people were forced to adopt the religion and languages of their conquerors. In the early 1800s most countries, inspired by the Venezuelan general, Simón Bolívar, and the Argentine general José de San Martin, fought for and achieved freedom from colonial rule. But frequent revolutions held back development.

Wars occurred between countries, and military groups often overthrew elected governments. Elected leaders, such as Juan Domingo Perón of Argentina, became dictators. The wealthy few held on to their land while millions lived in poverty. Many South American countries are deeply in debt but political stability is now helping industry to develop, and land reforms are reducing poverty.

**European colonies in 1790**

- Spanish
- Portuguese
- Dutch
- French

PARAGUAY 1811 — Present-day country borders and their dates of independence

VENEZUELA 1830
GUYANA 1966
SURINAM 1975
FRENCH GUIANA (French department since 1946)
COLOMBIA 1819
ECUADOR 1830
PERU 1821
BRAZIL 1822
BOLIVIA 1825
PARAGUAY 1811
CHILE 1818
ARGENTINA 1816
URUGUAY 1828
Falkland Islands (claimed by Britain in 1832)

### Important dates

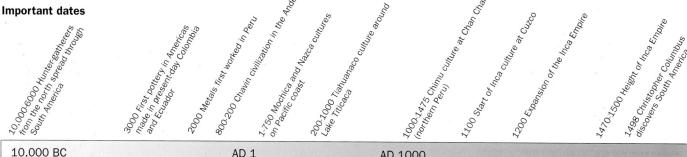

10,000-6000 Hunter-gatherers from the north spread through South America

3000 First pottery in Americas made in present-day Colombia and Ecuador

2000 Metals first worked in Peru

800-200 Chavín civilization in the Andes

1-750 Mochica and Nazca cultures on Pacific coast

200-1000 Tiahuanaco culture around Lake Titicaca

1000-1475 Chimu culture at Chan Chan (northern Peru)

1100 Start of Inca culture at Cuzco

1200 Expansion of the Inca Empire

1470-1500 Height of Inca Empire

1498 Christopher Columbus discovers South America

| 10,000 BC | | AD 1 | | AD 1000 | |
| --- | --- | --- | --- | --- | --- |

# ANTARCTICA

# ANTARCTICA AND ISLANDS

To the east of southern Argentina lie the Falkland Islands, which are geographically part of South America. The southernmost tip of South America is Cape Horn. South of the cape lies a stormy stretch of water called the Drake Passage, which is about 640km (about 400miles) wide. This passage separates South America from Antarctica, the fifth largest continent.

Antarctica is larger than Europe or Australia, but it has no permanent population. This is because it is bitterly cold and mostly covered by a huge ice sheet, up to about 4,800m (15,700ft) thick.

## ANTARCTICA
**Area**: about 14,000,000sq km (about 5,400,000sq miles)
**Highest point**: Vinson Massif 5,140m (16,864ft)
**Population**: none permanent

## FALKLAND ISLANDS
**Area**: 12,173sq km (4,700sq miles)
**Population**: 3,000
**Capital**: Stanley
**Government**: British overseas territory

**Falkland Islands** This territory, which consists of two large islands, East and West Falkland, and many small ones, is a British overseas territory, though Argentina claims the islands, which it calls Islas Malvinas. In April 1982, Argentine forces invaded the Falkland Islands. But Britain regained control in June when Argentina surrendered.

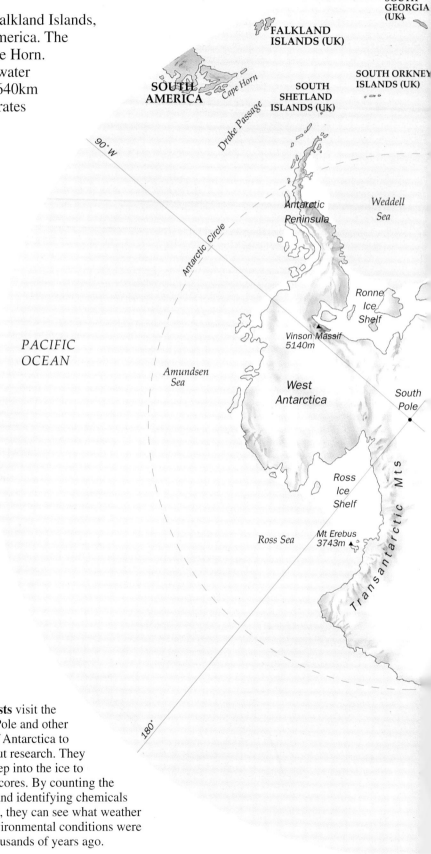

**Scientists** visit the South Pole and other parts of Antarctica to carry out research. They drill deep into the ice to collect cores. By counting the layers and identifying chemicals in them, they can see what weather and environmental conditions were like thousands of years ago.

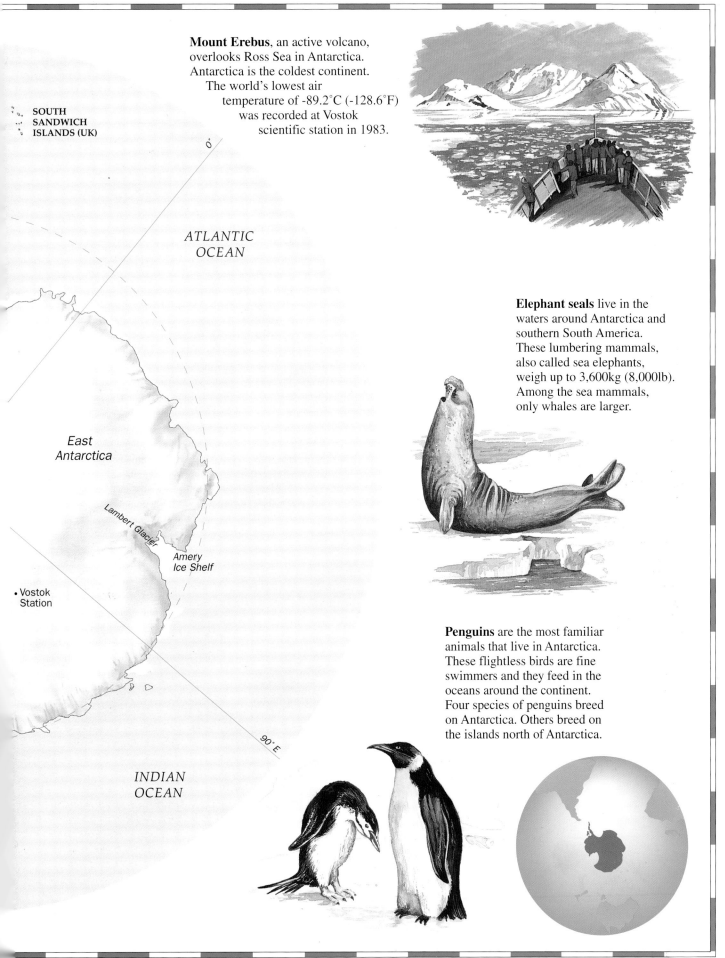

**Mount Erebus**, an active volcano, overlooks Ross Sea in Antarctica. Antarctica is the coldest continent. The world's lowest air temperature of -89.2°C (-128.6°F) was recorded at Vostok scientific station in 1983.

SOUTH
SANDWICH
ISLANDS (UK)

0°

ATLANTIC
OCEAN

East
Antarctica

Lambert Glacier

Amery
Ice Shelf

Vostok
Station

90°E

INDIAN
OCEAN

**Elephant seals** live in the waters around Antarctica and southern South America. These lumbering mammals, also called sea elephants, weigh up to 3,600kg (8,000lb). Among the sea mammals, only whales are larger.

**Penguins** are the most familiar animals that live in Antarctica. These flightless birds are fine swimmers and they feed in the oceans around the continent. Four species of penguins breed on Antarctica. Others breed on the islands north of Antarctica.

# ANTARCTICA AND ITS EXPLORATION

Antarctica was the last continent to be explored. The British Captain James Cook explored the southern oceans in the 18th century. He crossed the Antarctic Circle, but he did not sight land. The first men to walk on the continent were probably seal and whale hunters in the early 19th century.

American, French and British expeditions charted parts of the coast around 1840. One important expedition was led by James Clark Ross. He reached what is now the Ross Sea and he discovered two volcanoes which he named Erebus and Terror. These were the names of his ships.

The exploration of the interior of Antarctica did not begin until the early 1900s. In 1911, two men set out to reach the South Pole. The Norwegian Roald Amundsen reached the Pole on 14 December 1911. He and his companions returned safely. The British explorer Robert Falcon Scott reached the Pole just over a month later but all the members of his ill-equipped expedition died on the return trip.

**Roald Amundsen** was the first man to reach the South Pole. The United States Amundsen-Scott Station at the Pole is named after him and his gallant rival, Robert Falcon Scott, who also reached the Pole but died on the way home.

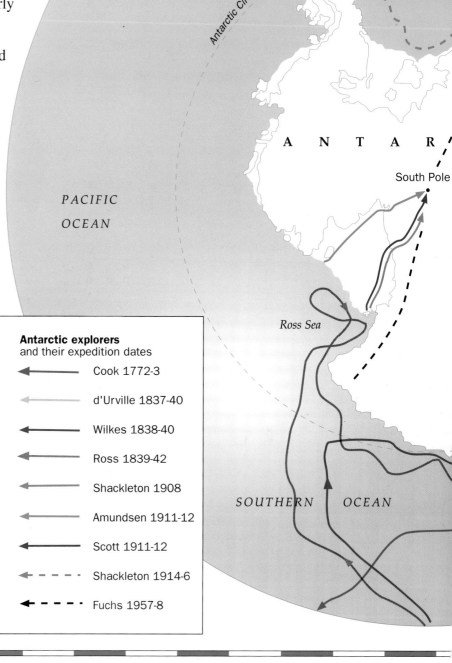

**Antarctic explorers**
and their expedition dates

| | |
|---|---|
| ← | Cook 1772-3 |
| ← | d'Urville 1837-40 |
| ← | Wilkes 1838-40 |
| ← | Ross 1839-42 |
| ← | Shackleton 1908 |
| ← | Amundsen 1911-12 |
| ← | Scott 1911-12 |
| ←- - - | Shackleton 1914-6 |
| ←- - - | Fuchs 1957-8 |

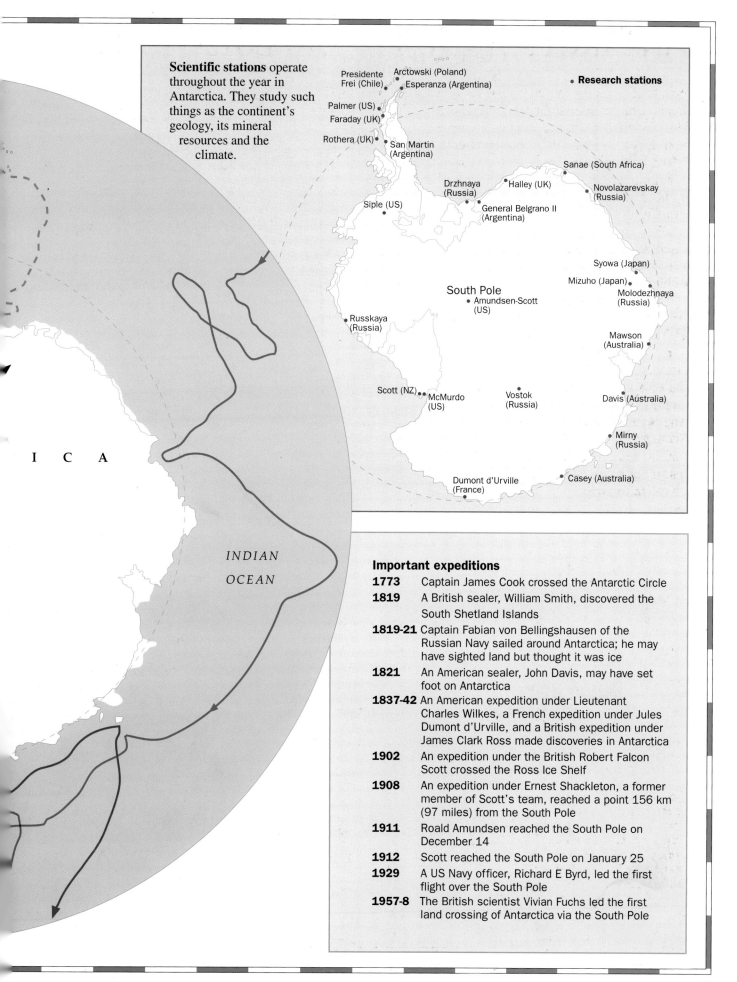

**Scientific stations** operate throughout the year in Antarctica. They study such things as the continent's geology, its mineral resources and the climate.

• **Research stations**

Presidente Frei (Chile)
Arctowski (Poland)
Esperanza (Argentina)
Palmer (US)
Faraday (UK)
Rothera (UK)
San Martin (Argentina)
Sanae (South Africa)
Drzhnaya (Russia)
Halley (UK)
Novolazarevskay (Russia)
Siple (US)
General Belgrano II (Argentina)
Syowa (Japan)
Mizuho (Japan)
Molodezhnaya (Russia)
South Pole
Amundsen-Scott (US)
Russkaya (Russia)
Mawson (Australia)
Scott (NZ)
McMurdo (US)
Vostok (Russia)
Davis (Australia)
Mirny (Russia)
Dumont d'Urville (France)
Casey (Australia)

I C A

*INDIAN OCEAN*

## Important expeditions

**1773**    Captain James Cook crossed the Antarctic Circle

**1819**    A British sealer, William Smith, discovered the South Shetland Islands

**1819-21**  Captain Fabian von Bellingshausen of the Russian Navy sailed around Antarctica; he may have sighted land but thought it was ice

**1821**    An American sealer, John Davis, may have set foot on Antarctica

**1837-42**  An American expedition under Lieutenant Charles Wilkes, a French expedition under Jules Dumont d'Urville, and a British expedition under James Clark Ross made discoveries in Antarctica

**1902**    An expedition under the British Robert Falcon Scott crossed the Ross Ice Shelf

**1908**    An expedition under Ernest Shackleton, a former member of Scott's team, reached a point 156 km (97 miles) from the South Pole

**1911**    Roald Amundsen reached the South Pole on December 14

**1912**    Scott reached the South Pole on January 25

**1929**    A US Navy officer, Richard E Byrd, led the first flight over the South Pole

**1957-8**  The British scientist Vivian Fuchs led the first land crossing of Antarctica via the South Pole

# ANTARCTICA TODAY

Although Antarctica is a cold and bleak place, it has many resources. For example, coal has been found in the continent. It was formed millions of years ago when Antarctica probably lay close to the equator and had a steamy, hot climate. Since then, Antarctica has slowly moved south to its present position around the South Pole.

### Climate and ice

Temperatures fall dramatically during the Antarctic winter which lasts from May to August. Icy winds, blowing at high speeds, make it feel even colder. In midsummer in January, temperatures reach 0°C (32°F) on the coast.

**Temperature in °C**

| | | | |
|---|---|---|---|
| ■ | -70° | ■ | -30° |
| ■ | -60° | ■ | -20° |
| ■ | -50° | ■ | -10° |
| ■ | -40° | □ | -4° |

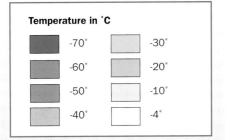

In winter the ice shelves extend to form floating pack ice that stretches 1,600km (1,000 miles) from the coast. In summer the ice breaks up to form flat icebergs, or ice floes. Recently huge icebergs the size of a small country have broken off. Some scientists think this may be the result of global warming which may be melting the ice shelves around the continent and causing an increase in snowfall. The melting or partial melting of the Antarctic ice sheet could raise sea levels around the world by between 5 and 20m (16 to 66 ft), submerging many islands and coastal areas.

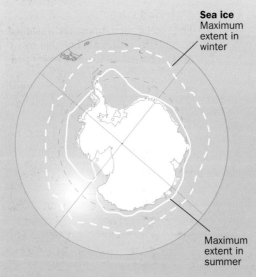

**Sea ice**
Maximum extent in winter

Maximum extent in summer

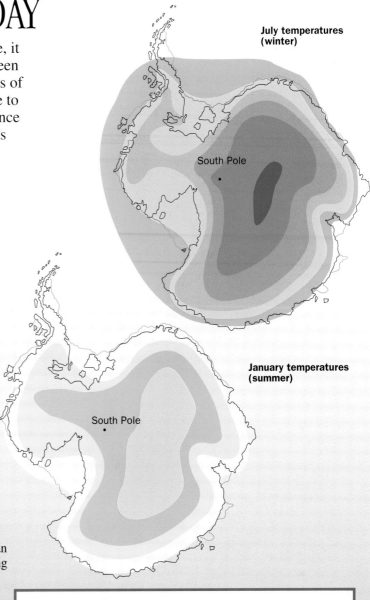

**July temperatures (winter)**

South Pole

**January temperatures (summer)**

South Pole

### The ozone hole

In the mid-1980s, scientists in Antarctica discovered that the ozone layer over Antarctica was being thinned by pollution, creating an 'ozone hole'. By 1998, the 'hole' covered an area about three times as large as the United States.

The ozone layer, between 12 and 24km (7.5 to 15 miles) above the earth, protects the land from the sun's harmful ultraviolet rays, which can cause skin cancer and damage to crops. A ban by many countries on the use of the chemicals that cause the damage has resulted in a reduced rate of destruction.

## Exploiting Antarctica

Geologists have discovered deposits of valuable minerals in Antarctica. At present, they are too expensive to mine and ship out from the icy continent. However, when supplies in the rest of the world become scarce, then mining companies might want to exploit them. Many people believe that mining would harm Antarctica and so mining is now banned.

Seven countries have claimed parts of Antarctica in the hope that, one day, they will be able to exploit its resources. However, the claims shown on the map, below, are not recognized in international law. Nations with an interest in Antarctica have signed treaties concerning the continent. For example, the Antarctic Treaty of 1959 states that the continent must be used only for peaceful purposes. It forbids the testing of nuclear weapons and the dumping of nuclear wastes. In 1991, it was also agreed that the exploitation of minerals should be banned for 50 years. This agreement came into force in 1998.

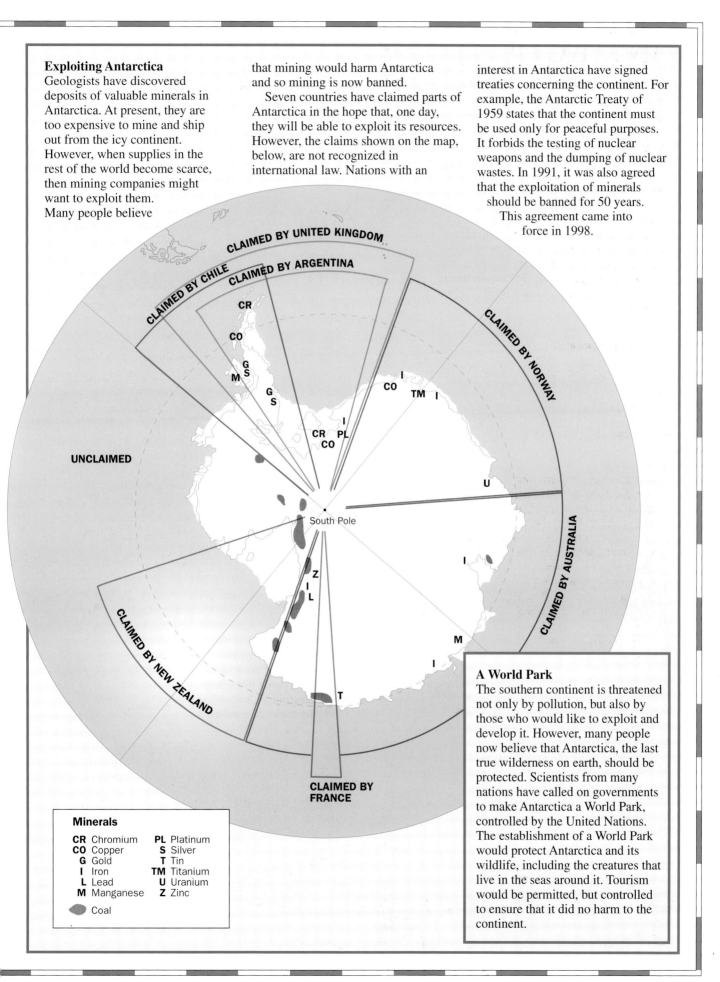

CLAIMED BY UNITED KINGDOM

CLAIMED BY CHILE

CLAIMED BY ARGENTINA

CLAIMED BY NORWAY

UNCLAIMED

South Pole

CLAIMED BY AUSTRALIA

CLAIMED BY NEW ZEALAND

CLAIMED BY FRANCE

### Minerals

| | | | |
|---|---|---|---|
| **CR** | Chromium | **PL** | Platinum |
| **CO** | Copper | **S** | Silver |
| **G** | Gold | **T** | Tin |
| **I** | Iron | **TM** | Titanium |
| **L** | Lead | **U** | Uranium |
| **M** | Manganese | **Z** | Zinc |

Coal

### A World Park

The southern continent is threatened not only by pollution, but also by those who would like to exploit and develop it. However, many people now believe that Antarctica, the last true wilderness on earth, should be protected. Scientists from many nations have called on governments to make Antarctica a World Park, controlled by the United Nations. The establishment of a World Park would protect Antarctica and its wildlife, including the creatures that live in the seas around it. Tourism would be permitted, but controlled to ensure that it did no harm to the continent.

# INDEX

**Picture credits**
**Photographs;** A S Publishing 8
Bernard Stonehouse 39
The Hutchison Library 5, 6, 7, 9, 13, 15, 17, 23, 26, 32-3
Travel Photo International 19, 21, 25,